ASSESSMENT SERIES

Series Editor
Jacalyn Lea Lund, Ph.D.
Georgia State University

Assessment of Swimming in Physical Education

Susan J. Grosse, MS

National Association for Sport and Physical Education
an association of the American Alliance for
Health, Physical Education, Recreation and Dance

Address orders to: AAHPERD Publications, P.O. Box 385, Oxon Hill, MD 20750-0385, or
call 1-800-321-0789. Order Stock No. 304-10301.

ISBN: 0-88314-912-5

Printed in the United States of America.

Suggested citation for this book:

Grosse, S. J. (2005). *Assessment of swimming in physical education.* Reston, VA: Author.

CONTENTS

155.42223 PIP

Lanchester Library

Learning, Research and Information Excellence

PREFACE

Assessment is an instructional tool that is finally coming into its own. For years, assessment was something that teachers tacked onto a unit at the completion of instruction, usually because they were required to give students a grade on their report cards. The educational reform movement helped escalate the attention given to assessments and moved them onto center stage. Requiring students to reach standards in various subject areas meant that teachers needed effective methods to measure learning. In a movement parallel with the development of standards, evaluation experts began calling for the development of authentic assessments (Wiggins, 1989). These new tests resembled work that adults, who were experts in the field, would be required to perform. Physical education had a relatively easy time adopting these new assessment formats because of its performance-based nature.

Assessment has matured with its purpose becoming to enhance student learning rather than merely measure it. Teachers use formative assessments on a regular basis to promote student learning. Incomplete learning and student misunderstandings are uncovered early enough in the instructional process allowing teachers to address these errors and improve student learning. Assessment is now woven throughout the instruction rather than only taking place on one day of a unit. In many instances it is difficult to separate instruction from assessment. In addition, assessment is no longer something that only teachers can do. Students have opportunities to assess themselves, as well as their peers in order to provide feedback that will augment the learning process.

Effective teachers have found that assessments help make instruction more deliberate, forcing them to decide in advance what students really need to learn. Key concepts and essential questions are identified, making learning and assessment more focused. Teacher effectiveness is viewed in terms of what students have learned rather than by the teaching behaviors exhibited by teachers. The days of "teach, test, hope for the best" are moving behind us as the focus of instruction is now measured in terms of student performance.

New assessment formats give teachers additional lenses through which to view student learning. In physical education, this has meant an increase in the use of performance-based assessments. Performance-based assessments allow teachers to analyze critically what students have learned. Measuring student learning on a regular basis can provide benchmarks for students and allow them to see their progress toward meeting final criteria. An added benefit is that students find these assessments both engaging and challenging.

It is now possible in physical education to document higher-level thinking using the applied assessments. Teachers can determine whether students are able to evaluate, synthesize, and analyze information and therefore apply knowledge in a meaningful manner. Teachers are now developing assessments for the affective and cognitive domains. Although these domains were sometimes ignored in the past, they are now assessed in a variety of ways.

The NASPE Assessment Series was created to provide teachers with additional resources and strategies for assessing student learning. Physical education teachers now have a vehicle for sharing assessments with other teachers and are able to provide materials and ideas that work. By offering individual publications, teachers can select the topics and types of assessments that are most useful to them. The intent of the series is to provide teachers with effective ways to measure student learning. The Assessment Series has given teachers a variety of strategies for assessing whether students are meeting local, state, and national content standards and for determining whether they are physically educated. In this age of accountability, this series has become a valuable resource for augmenting and documenting student learning.

We hope you will enjoy this most recent addition to the NASPE Assessment Series and find it useful in your work. These books are developed for physical educators in schools and for faculty preparing prospective physical education teachers. The manuscripts undergo a rigorous review process to ensure that they are of the highest quality and will be useful for teachers, teacher educators, and others engaged in the process of teaching physical activity to today's youth. The series represents cutting-edge ideas and allows readers to stay informed about the latest innovations in assessment. Our goal is to provide teachers with practical and innovative tools for successfully negotiating the challenges and changes associated with educational reform.

Jacalyn Lea Lund, Ph.D.

INTRODUCTION

"Can I go off the diving board?"
"When can I swim in deep water?"
"Why do I get so tired?"
"Why didn't my son/daughter pass swimming?"
"Just how good of a swimmer is my child?"
"What swim class comes next?"

These are just a few of the many questions physical education teachers are asked while teaching swimming. Instructors looking for answers to these and other questions can find those answers through assessments.

Students who develop swim skills may enjoy swimming for life. Assessment helps students develop those skills. To provide answers to the important questions above, as well as many others concerning knowledge, skill acquisition, and performance, instructors can use assessment to help students set goals and develop self-confidence when they meet those goals. Instructors can also use assessment results to plan appropriate class activities.

Assessment of Swimming in Physical Education provides a variety of assessment methods that physical education teachers can use to determine middle and high school students' abilities. The methods emphasize skilled swimming development and water safety. Students who attain swimming skills have "access to the tremendous variety inherent in the activity (of swimming) for a lifetime of physical fitness" (McEvoy, 1993, p. 1). Safety is a vital part of swimming instruction; therefore, assessments of water safety skills are also included here for instructor use.

PART 1

Student Assessment, Swimming, and the NASPE Standards

Assessment and Skilled Swimming

Assessment is the process of gathering evidence to determine progress toward student achievement (National Association for Sport and Physical Education [NASPE], 1995) Instructors can assess physical performance to determine skill acquisition through form and efficiency. In addition, teachers may want to assess students' knowledge to determine their understanding and ability to apply those skills.

Teachers can use the assessments in this book to assess isolated skills and provide feedback to students on their ability, skill levels, and safety knowledge. Water safety is important to reduce potential aquatic-related accidents and to increase student safety in the water.

Scope of Learning to Swim

In general, swim instructors will want to assess two general categories: form and function. Colvin states, "efficient technique is concerned mainly with increasing propulsion while decreasing the resistance of the water to the swimmer's forward movement" (1992, p. 3). Swimmers' style and form directly relate to their success. Therefore, instructors will want to focus on correct form, because it increases swimmers' skills.

Various national organizations, including the American Red Cross (2004b) and the YMCA of the USA (1999), have quantified swimming skills assessments. Their programs have progressive, sequential accomplishment levels, all of which include assessment as a foundation for progression. However, not all physical education teachers are Red Cross or YMCA certified instructors. Additionally, not all physical education swim programs have a national level curriculum base. The assessments included in this book link instruction and assessment for virtually any swim program. Teachers can apply these assessments to several different types of swim skills and stroke components.

NASPE Standards

Swimming skills directly support standards 1 through 6 of the National Standards for Physical Education (NASPE, 2004). Instructors may want to consider the following examples:

Standard 1: *Demonstrates competency in motor skills and movement patterns needed to perform a variety of physical activities.*

To acquire swim skills, students must develop unique movement patterns. Once these patterns are established, swimmers gain access to a broader motor skill repertoire. Once students develop the motor skills associated with swimming and locomotion in water, they can participate in a variety of additional activities. Assessment provides teachers and students with a reference point for their accomplishment levels and their readiness for other aquatic activities. Instructors who assess skills, both in isolation and in combination with other skills, can document skill development and its application to movement concepts. Scenario assessments enable teachers to gauge students' abilities to apply their knowledge during real-life circumstances.

Standard 2: *Demonstrates understanding of movement concepts, principles, strategies, and tactics as they apply to the learning and performance of physical activities.*

Out of the water, students' bodies move under the influence of gravity and maintain their balance around a center of gravity. In water, buoyancy negates the effects of gravity. Without the pull of gravity, movement in water is different than movement on land and buoyancy facilitates activity. Therefore, water movement is different and unique from other athletic endeavors. Teachers can help students apply the mechanical principles of how the body functions in water. In addition, instructors can help students learn how to use their arms and legs in water and to balance despite continually changing water pressure.

Standard 3: *Participates regularly in physical activity.*

Swimming can be a lifetime activity. For students to become regular participants, they must want to swim and have the opportunity to participate. When teachers provide swimming assessments that help students develop their skills, students are more likely to want to continue swimming for the rest of their lives.

As an individual sport, swimming only requires water, which is readily available in pools, lakes, rivers, and oceans. Equipment is not necessary. Virtually everyone can swim regardless of age, general physical condition, or disability.

Standard 4: *Achieves and maintains a health-enhancing level of physical fitness.*

When swimmers move through water, they encounter resistance, which develops their strength. In addition, swimmers' flexibility is improved, which causes increased range of motion. Muscular endurance increases as swimmers extend the length of their activities. Most importantly, swimming improves circulation and aerobic capacity. Maximum fitness benefits are possible when students swim with optimal efficiency.

Standard 5: *Exhibits responsible personal and social behavior that respects self and others in physical activity settings.*

Swim instructors who help young people develop water safety knowledge and skills enable students to save their own lives or the lives of others. When students learn to recognize danger, plan for emergencies, and follow safety precautions, they typically become more responsible. Students who rescue other swimmers show the ultimate act of responsible behavior.

Standard 6: *Values physical activity for health, enjoyment, challenge, self-expression, and/or social interaction.*

Aquatic activities, like other physical education activities, support this standard. Swimming offers unique opportunities to students who are not successful in land activities. Students who do not exhibit mobility, speed, or agility on land might excel in swimming.

When instructors help students become competent swimmers they are teaching students to value swimming as a lifetime activity. Aquatic activities contain many challenges. Accomplishment of these challenges develops self-confidence and esteem. Meeting these challenges alongside their peers enhances social interaction, as all participants deal with similar problems and work toward common goals. Students value activities in which they can grow and swimming provides an unparalleled potential for growth.

PART 2

Methods of Assessment

Each type of assessment presented in this book has a place in a swim curriculum. Instructors can determine which assessment to use based on their program goals and objectives, as well as students' needs and interests. Some assessments—including form assessments, skill checklists, combined skill tests/applications, and written tests—are usually teacher assessments in which teachers provide the primary opinion regarding assessment results. Other assessments—including precourse, scenarios, journaling, and teach backs—are student assessments. In these assessments, students provide assessments of skill and feedback.

Assessments can measure form, skill application, knowledge, behavior, attitude, or decision making (Table 1). It is important to assess all areas of growth and development toward skilled swimming, since they all interact with each other in regard to participation in aquatic activities. The chart below can help instructors select assessments based on their goals for assessment.

No single assessment provides teachers with all the information they need to analyze swim skills and knowledge completely. No matter what type of assessment an instructor uses, teachers and students should review and discuss the results together. This discussion provides a common understanding of goals and results. When assessing individual performance, discussion with the specific student being assessed helps clarify feedback. When assessing problem solving and/or decision making, students can benefit from group discussion and feedback, with all members of a peer group contributing to a final conclusion.

Reviewing assessments is particularly important for scenarios. Students and teachers both benefit from a joint analysis of students' responses, especially when instructors clarify fallacies in the decision-making process and/or conclusions reached. Anyone participating in the assessment process can also suggest safe alternatives.

Most assessments can be used for multiple purposes. Sample assessment documents included in this book give teachers a starting point from which they can customize their own assessments to fit specific swim activities and situational circumstances.

	Form	Skill	Knowledge	Behavior	Attitude	Decision Making
Form Assessments	X	X	X			
Precourse Assessments	X	X	X		X	X
Skill Checklists	X	X				
Combined Skill Tests/Applications		X	X	X		X
Written Tests			X		X	X
Scenarios			X		X	X
Journaling			X		X	X
Teach Backs		X	X	X	X	X

Table 1. Different Assessments and What They Measure

Precourse Assessments

Because of the differences between shallow water and deepwater swimming, it is critical for instructors to assess swimmers' entry-level experiences and capabilities. Precourse assessments are important for curriculum planning and goal setting, as well as for establishing and maintaining a safe environment.

A precourse assessment can help students clarify their prior experiences and abilities so they can make appropriate course selections. Precourse assessments can also provide teachers with information necessary to plan activities appropriate for students' needs and abilities. For example, instructional swimming is depth specific: entry-level stroke skills should be taught in shallow water, so tired swimmers can stand if necessary.

A typical Precourse Assessment Survey, which can be found in Appendix A, promotes reflective thinking on the students' part and allows teachers to gather information. The first part of the survey explains its use. Students can then select a statement to describe their prior experience and their ability to perform specific skills. Instructors can use the last section of the form to better understand student course selections. For example, a student might be able to swim in deep water, but elect to start at a fairly low level of skill development. Additional information provided by the student indicates that he cannot swim any of the specific strokes, but that he is merely a strong dog paddler. This information clarifies this student's need to begin at a lower instructional level. The survey should not impact student grades.

Teachers can use the Precourse Assessment Survey to assess students on the skills that each student believes they can perform. Instructors' comments, written directly on a student's survey sheet, can either confirm the student's self-assessments or add additional information to clarify student perceptions. Using the survey, the teacher affirms student performance levels or indicates, following in-water assessment, why students should reconsider course selection. If wide discrepancies exist between the teacher's and student's views, the teacher may want to hold a teacher-student conference.

This survey also gives students an opportunity to share additional information with the teacher, such as a fear of swimming or water, medical issues, the need to obtain proper attire, or other concerns. If all students complete the survey, no students will feel singled out. After completing the course,

students can fill out the survey a second time. Instructors can compare pre- and post-course skills to validate assessment results. Teachers may want to place the assessments in each student's physical education portfolio.

Form Assessments

Performance efficiency relies on form; therefore it is critical for instructors to assess stroke form as part of swim-skill assessments. Colvin (1992, p. 16) breaks down assessment of form using the following questions:

- When and how should the hand(s) enter the water?
- Should the arm(s) be bent or straight during the pull?
- What path should the arm(s) take during the pull?
- Should the stroke be long and slow or short and fast?
- How should the arm(s) be brought forward to start the next stroke?
- How should the timing of one arm relate to the other?
- How should leg timing relate to the arms?

In order for form assessment to take place, teachers must compare a swimmer's performance with their mental pictures of efficient skill performance. The American Red Cross (2004a) considers this ability critical for teachers and refers to it as a *photographic eye*.

Once instructors have compared a swimmer's actual stroke form to the desired stroke, instructors should provide feedback to students. Teachers can provide verbal feedback to students, but this may not be the best way, because swimmers sometimes get water in their ears and have difficulty hearing due to pool noise and other distractions. Thomas (1989) recommends handing out assessment sheets at the start of a course. This gives students an idea of what is expected and becomes the basis for later comparison. A Form Assessment Chart (Appendix B) is an example of an assessment sheet.

When using the Form Assessment Chart for in-water assessment, teachers use one chart for each student. While watching the student swim, teachers write directly on the chart. In the "Stroke" column, teachers can check "pass" if the swimmer's stroke is acceptable for that skill level. Additional positive and constructive comments can be helpful too. If form errors occur, instructors can check or circle the specific stroke component that needs improvement. For example, a check next to rhythmic breathing would indicate to the student that an error occurred. Teachers can either write on the form about how to correct the error or meet with students to provide more specific information. For example, to address a swimmer with a rhythmic breathing problem, the teacher's note could say, "breathe every stroke." In order to provide updates of student progress and changes in skill development, teachers could continue to use this chart by writing with different color inks. Short descriptions in the stroke component columns can vary with the level at which the chart is being used. The content of the chart in Appendix B is appropriate for higher levels of stroke form.

Instructors may choose to use the more open-ended Skill Evaluation Summary (see Figure 1, which provides some examples of the type of feedback teachers can provide on Skill Evaluation Summary cards) instead of the Form Assessment Chart. With the Skill Evaluation Summary, teachers view swimmers and write comments on the particular stroke or skill. This format allows students to focus on fewer comments at one time, which is particularly helpful for students with learning disabilities. Teachers must point out errors and provide necessary corrections. The summary could be preprinted on note cards and teachers could give each student a pack of blank cards similar to the first card in Figure 1. Having students keep cards in their own possession places responsibility for timely assessments on the student. Students who feel they are ready to be assessed can give a card to the teacher at the beginning of class, be assessed

Name		Date	
Stroke/Skill			
Arms			
Legs			
Coordination			
Breathing			

Name	Jane Swimmer	Date	May 8
Stroke/Skill	Front Crawl		
Arms	Reach further forward before entry; pull closer under center of body		
Legs	Good, kick is steady		
Coordination	Good		
Breathing	Remember to take breath on every stroke		

Name	Jane Swimmer	Date	~~May 8~~ 5/15
Stroke/Skill	Front Crawl		
Arms	~~Reach further forward before entry; pull closer under center of body~~ Much		
Legs	Good, kick is steady		Improved
Coordination	Good		
Breathing	~~Remember to take breath on every stroke~~ Yes, nice!		

Figure 1. Skill Evaluation Summary

during a specific part of class, and then get the card back from the teacher at the end of class. If the skill is completed successfully, it is so noted on the card. The teacher makes a record of the accomplishment in his or her grade book, and the student keeps the card as a record for her or himself. If re-assessment is needed, the student gives the same card to the teacher at the time of the next assessment. The teacher can see comments from prior assessments and not only add current comments, but also determine the rate of progress.

Form assessments should include an assessment of body position, as it will give teachers an indication that something is wrong with the stroke. Body position is not the problem, but rather a consequence of the problem. Although body position and alignment are not included on either form assessment sample, instructors should realize that body position, which is often dictated by head position and arm/leg action, can be assessed this way. For example, when swimmers perform the front crawl without placing their entire faces in the water they have greater resistance because their legs are below the horizontal plane of the upper body. This, in turn, weakens the kick and makes out-of-water arm recovery more difficult. Body roll will be compromised and swimmers usually will fatigue faster. To provide corrective feedback on head position, teachers can tell swimmers, "when you blow bubbles, place your entire face (up to just past the eyebrows) into the water and point your nose toward the bottom of the pool." After hearing this feedback, students can align their heads correctly by lowering them into the water. This will likely improve overall body position—the legs will rise and the swimmers' bodies will become more horizontal. Swimmers will then experience easier arm recovery and generally perform a more efficient front crawl.

Swim instructors should add or delete any categories and change any descriptions they feel necessary to implement their swimming assessments.

Skill Checklists

Checklists are common in swimming, especially in national learn-to-swim programs. There are several different types of aquatic skill checklists that can be found in Appendix C, beginning with an Aquatic Skills Progression Chart. The Aquatic Skills Progression Chart lists a multitude of skills commonly found in learn-to-swim programs. Instructors can use this chart as a whole or create shorter checklists

from this chart, such as the Safety/Self Rescue Skills Progression Chart. The Safety/Self Rescue Skills Progression Chart, which can also be found in Appendix C, is an example of how a specific category of skills and component parts of skills can be detailed for assessment purposes. Sometimes students need skills broken into smaller segments. For example, skill in elementary rescue is really many different subsets of skills—reaching assists, throwing assists, and wading assists. Each of these subsets can further be broken apart into more individual skills. Reaching assists, for example, include pole, towel, rescue tube, and arm/leg extensions. Isolating skill categories from the Aquatic Skills Progression Chart and making specific skill progression charts for a particular skill can facilitate student focus and aid in assessment.

Teachers can use the space at the top of each column to customize the chart for the different skill levels or classes: numbers (e.g., level 1, 2, 3, indicating levels of accomplishment), letters for grades that can be earned (e.g., A level, B level, C level), descriptors (e.g., beginner, intermediate), or something non-evaluative (e.g., red, blue, green).

If instructors give each student a checklist, such as the Aquatic Skill Progression Chart, students can check off skills as they learn them. Teachers can also collect the checklists from the students, use the checklists for performance evaluations (by writing or checking off items on the checklist), and then return them to the students. In this situation, teachers would mark the specific skills that students performed correctly. To assess and chart the progress of a large group of students, instructors can use a variation of the Master Skill Checklist (Appendix C), which lists skills across the top of the grid and student names along the right side.

All students should have copies of the assessments used in class. These help students set goals and focus their attention on specific skills. A good checklist represents skill-development progressions.

Instructors should organize items on the list in the order in which students will learn the skills. Skill checklists can also contain contents grouped by the type of aquatic activity, with swim skills in one section and safety skills in another. Table 2, on the following page, has three categories of skills: stroke skills, elementary rescues, and survival skills. The numbers in the left column indicate the order in which skills will be taught. While a student might not gain mastery in this order, the order can assist in teaching progression.

Students can see their growth in skill mastery, as additional items are accomplished and checked

	Stroke Skills	Elementary Rescue Skills	Survival Skills
1	Front kick glide	Reaching assist with pole	Bobs and bubbles 10 times
2	Front crawl arms	Reaching assist with arm/leg	Survival float in five feet of water
3	Combined crawl kick and arms	Reaching assist with rescue towel	Tread water in six feet of water, near side of pool
4	Rhythmic breathing to side with crawl kick and arms	Reaching assist with rescue tube	

*Note: Numbers do not indicate order of difficulty. They are merely place holders to assist in using this form.

Table 2. Skill Checklist

off. Teachers may want to have sublists on the checklist as well. For example, if the front crawl is listed as an individual skill, sublists of the kick, arm stroke, breathing, and coordination will help students identify all the skill components they need to master that stroke. Sample charts and checklists included in Appendix C contain a mix of swim skills and safety practices. Instructors can modify the lists depending on the swim course curriculum.

Teachers should not use even the best skill checklist as their sole assessment for swim class. Checklists usually help assess the process or form elements of a skill and instructors should use other types of assessments for more complex assessments.

Combined Skill Tests/Applications.

Combined skill tests or skill applications enable teachers to assess a sequence of skills, which are performed under conditions that closely simulate how swimmers would use them outside the class. Assessing isolated skills gives an incomplete indication of actual swim ability. A swimmer's performance in water usually includes a combination of breath control, balance, change of direction, response to buoyancy, and variable mobility; therefore, teachers' assessment of a skill must include consideration of all of these factors. The Combined Skill Assessment Matrix (Table 3) can help in making sure all performance components

	Needs Additional Practice	Making Progress	Accomplished
Breath Control	Coughed. Swallowed water. Nose full of water.	Held breath.	Demonstrated appropriate inhale/exhale pattern.
Balance	Body rolled excessively; poor body position.	Body moved in and out of stable position.	Maintained appropriate body roll and stability throughout
Change of Direction	Stood up or grabbed wall.	Made wide turn. Swam excessively.	Turned efficiently— appropriate to skill level.
Response to Buoyancy	Struggled to maintain surface position.	Maintained appropriate appropriate position with someadditional movement.	Maintained skill appropriate position with little extra effort.
Variable Mobility	Unable to vary pace. Maintained slow pace.	Began at appropriate pace, but did not maintain pace over time. Changed direction with decreasing difficulty.	Adjusted pace as circumstances demanded. Varied pace to accommodate change of direction.

Table 3. Combined Skill Assessment Matrix

are included in assessment. To assess whether students can apply skills in a real-world setting the assessment would measure students jumping in, surfacing, changing direction, and then swimming a short distance to safety.

By combining skills in authentic sequences, instructors have the opportunity to assess students' skill applications. Combined skill tests and applications help students bridge the gap between checklist assessments and real-life application of skills. Instructors teach their students additional swimming skills when they complete Combined Skill Tests/Applications, as found in Appendix D, which represent a variety of situations, as well as students' functional levels of ability.

In order to assess a skill combination, instructors should be sure that students, prior to performance, understand the combination by asking them to repeat the skill sequence verbally. For some students, particularly students with learning disabilities, not understanding swimming terminology inhibits their performance. Remember that the order of a skill-combination sequence is difficult for some students. Instructors can provide verbal prompts during students' performances to help them. Remember, the prompt should provide sequence, not how the sequence should be performed. For example, a student being asked to jump in, swim 10 yards to a cone marker, turn around, and swim back to the start may need to be prompted to "jump," "swim," "turn," and "swim" to cue him or her about the sequence. Adding information on how to swim or turn would provide information the student should be able to demonstrate as part of the assessment. For beginning swimmers, the ability to combine skills should be the focus of the assesment, rather than their language or memory abilities.

To assess combinations, instructors may want to focus on two different components: performance of each skill and transition from skill to skill. If students stop or take a break during transitions or are unable to perform a skill, they need to work on all parts of the combination. Teachers can use a Skill Combination Performance Card (Figure 2) to document the results of a student's combined skill-test performance. Students can fill in their name and the date and the combination components to be assessed. Teachers can check off component parts or mark whether students "pass" or "complete" the skill, before returning cards to students.

Written Tests

A longtime staple of the education system, written tests document students' cognitive knowledge. In addition, written tests provide legal documentation of material students receive regarding the parameters of safe participation. When students write their answers on a test, those answers document whether the student knows the correct information. This documentation is critical for instructors. Negligence suits (Bayless & Adams, 1985; Meeks, 1990) repeatedly cite teachers' failure to warn of dangers. Written tests can help teachers avoid legal action by documenting the teachers' warnings, as well as students' comprehension of those warnings.

For documentation purposes, written tests in instructional swim classes should include the following:

- Questions that require students to provide content answers. For example,

  Question: What is the minimum water depth for diving safely from a deck?

  Answer: Nine feet.

- Questions that do not have a high-guess factor. If teachers choose to include true/fale questions, students should be required to correct the false statements. For example,

  Question: Seven feet is the minimum water depth for diving safely from a deck.

  Answer: False, the minimum depth for diving safely from a deck is nine feet.

- Multiple-choice questions with possible answers that are all believable. For example,

  Question: Which stroke has a glide?
  a.   front crawl
  b.   sidestroke
  c.   butterfly
  d.   back crawl

  Answer: b. sidestroke

  These are far better choices than having "a. dolphin kick, b. sidestroke, c. back crawl, and d. surface dive" as possible answers, because the latter are not all believable answers. Choices a and d, which are not strokes, are clearly incorrect, and option c is questionable, which leaves b as the obvious answer.

- Questions that ask students to state what appropriate behavior is, as opposed to stating what not to do. For example,

  Question: If a swimmer is tired, a good stroke to use is the _____.

Answer: Elementary backstroke.

A "not" question (e.g., What stroke is not good to swim when tired?") might result in the answer "front crawl," as well as possibly several other answers. Teachers who ask what *should* be done will have a better idea about whether a student understands a concept.

It is important for students to see the results of their written tests. Instructors should make sure that students correct their answers, either through class discussion or by rewriting the question and

correct answer in a positive statement. Students who did not pass the written test should be given study time before taking a different version of the same test. A retest documents correction of faulty knowledge. Students who cannot pass a written test—on safety or any other swim component—in swim class lack the information and understanding they need to participate safely. When students correct their misinformation, they have a better understanding of the sound educational practices in aquatics.

Once students have seen their results, teachers

Card A: Blank assessment card

| Name | | Date | |
| Combination | | | Teacher Comments: |

Card B: As completed by student, prior to assessment

Name	Jane Swimmer	Date	May 9
Combination #	#3 - jump into deep water		Teacher Comments:
	swim front crawl 10 yards		
	reverse direction		
	swim back crawl to return to start		

Card C: With comments by teacher, following performance by student

Name	Jane Swimmer	Date	May 9
Combination #	#3 - jump into deep water		Teacher Comments:
	swim front crawl 10 yards		Must repeat – don't grab wall during reverse
	reverse direction		
	swim back crawl to return to start		

Figure 2. Skill Combination Performance Cards

should keep all the students' tests on file. The tests, along with the students' answers, are proof that the instructors taught the students the material. When students retake tests that they have previously failed, instructors have documentation to show that students were warned of participation hazards and that they had the opportunity to learn how to participate safely.

Teachers should give a written test right after they present preliminary safety precautions to the class. Appendix E contains a sample written test on safety and pool rules knowledge. Another sample written test, one that documents swimming skills, is also found in Appendix E.

Scenarios

Decision making is difficult to assess. Instructors need to consider the best way to determine whether students can apply what they have learned to real-life decision-making situations. Physical educators can use written and water scenarios to assess their students' decision-making skills. Scenarios also enable teachers to give students feedback regarding the consequences of their decisions. In addition, scenarios allow students to explore additional decision alternatives and their outcomes. If scenarios are written with the eventual outcome undecided, students can explore a variety of options and the behaviors associated with them.

Scenarios allow a variety of assessments: pairs of students assessing each other, groups of students assessing individuals, or teachers providing feedback to groups, pairs, or individuals. Each version has its advantages and disadvantages. Teens, in particular, often value peer opinion over what adults have to say. This is particularly true when discussing personal experiences. A friend telling a friend they can improve a swim stroke by kicking faster may generate more skill improvement than a teacher saying the same thing. Perception affects performance. For some teens, friends help, teachers correct. Instructors can gain valuable insight to teens' thought processes by listening to peer commentary. This invaluable information can help teachers develop future lesson plans. Figure 3 includes samples of written and water scenarios that instructors can use in their classes.

Journaling

Self-assessment is the primary purpose of journaling. When students are learning to swim, they need to be able to estimate their personal abilities accurately. While some students will have advanced skills and comprehensive knowledge, many others will enter the swim class with no prior experience. Students need to analyze their swim class experiences in order to gain a perspective on their capabilities in relation to their environments.

By keeping a journal, students can gain perspective on their swimming abilities, re-assessing themselves as progress is noted. Students also have an emotional outlet to express their feelings. It is easier for students to cope with fear and uncertainty if they are able to express and quantify their feelings. For example, if a teacher asks students why they are hesitant to jump into deep water, the students might respond with "I don't know." However, if those students keep a journal, they can see their own progress. Seeing progress helps lessen fear because accomplishment can be empowering. Once progress is noted, fearful students learn that water is not something they need to be afraid of and they are then able to learn how to swim. Students can also work through their fears by planning ahead for particular activities. Instructors may ask students to write on any topic they wish, as long as the journal entry relates to the activity for that day. Teachers can initiate a prompted writing by supplying a question or statement, such as the following:

- What is the most important thing you have learned in this class so far and why?
- What skills do you think should be learned before swimming in deep water?
- Learning to swim is _____. Complete this statement and explain your answer.
- Based on my skill level, the skills I would like to learn are _____. Give your answers and explain why.
- If you could learn any new aquatic activity, what would it be? Why? What skills would you need in order to learn the activity?
- What safety advice would you give someone going to a waterpark for the first time?
- What scares you most about jumping into deep water for the first time? How will you meet this challenge?
- How many classes do you think it will take for you to learn how to swim to the bottom of a 10-foot deep pool? How will you practice to get there?
- What new skills did you learn today and why was it important to learn them?

Water Scenarios

Teachers read the scenarios aloud to students, and then watch and assess their performances. In assessing performance, first determine if the set-up is correct and the situation is enacted appropriately. If so, then consider the following questions:

- Were helping actions appropriate to the circumstance?
- Were helping actions performed correctly?
- Were all actions performed safely?

Set-up: *Students in pairs in shallow water. One student is the victim and the other is the helper.*
Situation: A swimmer near you is very tired and cannot stand up. He or she is struggling and looks afraid.
Appropriate action: The helper should help the victim stand up and verbally reassure the victim.

Set-up: *Students in pairs. One student is the helper and is standing on the deck, the other student is in a lane.*
Situation: You are swimming a long distance and do not have a way to stand up and rest, nor do you have anything to hold on to in order to rest. Can you keep swimming until I blow the whistle [*Note to the teacher:* adjust the time to the level of the swimmers]? You may use any resting techniques you know, except for touching the side of the pool or standing up.
Appropriate action: The helper should watch the swimmer to remind him or her not to touch the walls or stand up. The helper can also suggest resting techniques such as survival float, alternating strokes, and/or back float (depending on lane traffic).

Set-up: *Students in groups of 4 or 5 in shallow water. One student is a younger child and the others are helpers.*
Situation: A child accidentally swims into water over his or her head. How can you work together, without any equipment, to assist the child?
Appropriate action: The helpers should make a human chain and perform a wading rescue using the human chain to extend an arm, leg, towel, or other object to the young child.

Set-up: *Students in pairs in shallow water. One student is the victim and the other is the helper.*
Situation: You are swimming alongside a friend when your friend says that he or she is very tired. What can you do, without touching your friend, to help?
Appropriate action: The helper should move away a little from the individual (i.e., out of reach) and tell the friend to roll over onto his or her back and rest. After the victim is able to take a brief rest, the helper gives his or her friend directions to kick and paddle gently, which conserves energy, and to turnover and swim back to safety.

Set-up: *A single student, swimming across the pool.*
Situation: The swimming student suddenly gets a cramp in his or her lower left leg.
Appropriate action: The student should initiate a survival float and massage out the cramp.

Written Scenarios

Students complete the written scenarios. In assessing writing, look for four paragraphs, one to answer each of the four questions in the assignment. Then evaluate the content of each paragraph for the following questions:

- Did the student understand what happened?
- Could the student tell how the circumstance could have been avoided?
- Did the student offer something they could have done?
- Did the student know what else could have been done to keep people safe?

Continues on page 14

Figure 3. Water and Written Scenarios

Continued from page 14

Lake Scenario

Read the following scenario and analyze what happened. Then write a report or be prepared to discuss the following questions:

◊ What actually happened?

◊ What would you have done if you had been there?

◊ How could the accident have been avoided?

◊ What could have been done to keep people from getting into life-threatening situation while swimming?

You and your friend are at the lake. It is a hot day and it is very crowded in the roped-off swim area. You need more room to really swim and have fun, so you and your friend move outside the roped area to where there is more room. You are having a great time, when your friend suddenly starts making small splashes and gurgling sounds. He is about 10 yards away and doesn't answer when you ask what is happening. As you move closer to him, the splashes subside a bit, but your friend still doesn't answer you. Just as you reach your friend, you feel the bottom drop away and you can no longer stand. Suddenly your friend grabs you hard. Both you and your friend sink under water. Pushing off the lake bottom, you struggle to get away. You manage to get back to where you can stand and realize that you cannot see your friend. People on the beach call for the lifeguard who quickly responds to the emergency and takes control of the situation.

Student responses should be assessed based on the following for each question:

✔ What actually happened? *Answer:* My friend and I went outside the swim area and he stepped off a drop-off or into a hole. I went to help him and he grabbed me. I got away and the lifeguard came to take over and began a search for my friend.

✔ How could the accident have been avoided? *Answer:* It could have been avoided if we had stayed in the designated swim area, checked the depth of the undesignated area before swimming there, and immediately called for help.

✔ What would you have done if you had been there? *Answer:* I would have stayed in the designated swim area, checked the depth of the water in the undesignated area, and called the lifeguard immediately.

✔ What could have been done to keep people from getting into a life-threatening while swimming? *Answer:* We could have stayed in the designated swim area.

River Scenario

Read the following scenario and analyze what happened. Then write a report or be prepared to discuss the following questions:

◊ What actually happened?

◊ What would you have done if you had been there?

◊ How could the accident have been avoided?

◊ What could have been done to keep people from getting into life-threatening situation while swimming?

You are with a group of friends at a riverfront park. There is no swim area, but people are in the river having a good time. You and your friends go in for a swim. Everyone is feeling great, the weather is perfect, and the water feels wonderful. As something to do, your group decides to swim across the river. It doesn't look far and you think you see more friends on the other shore. About two-thirds of the way across, you start to slow down. It must be farther across than you thought. You tell your friends to keep going and that you will catch up. But, they get farther and farther away and you start moving slower and slower until you are not moving at all. In fact, you can barely keep your head above water.

Student responses should be assessed based on the following for each question:

✔ What actually happened? *Answer:* We went swimming without a lifeguard. I overestimated my ability to swim across the river. I did not know how to rest while swimming. My friends left me.

✔ How could the accident have been avoided? *Answer:* It could have been avoided if I swam where a lifeguard was on duty, knew my ability level and made appropriate decisions, stayed with my friend, and knew how to rest when I was tired.

✔ What would.you have done if you had been there? *Answer:* I would have stayed out of the river, stayed close to the shore, used a buddy system, and rested on my back or with a survival float.

✔ What could have been done to keep people from getting into a life-threatening situation while swimming? *Answer:* We could have stayed out of the water, swam where a lifeguard was on duty, used a buddy system, stayed within our ability levels, and used proper resting positions/techniques.

Figure 3. Water and Written Scenarios continued

When teachers read journal entries, they must be very careful to respect students' privacy. The least intrusive method is to check only to see if the journal entry was made, trusting the students' thought processes. Reading the entries is more intrusive, but it is necessary to assess a student's information-processing skills. In addition, teachers can use the journal pages to write additional questions in the margins and/or make suggestions or comments for students to think about. Reading journal entries also provides general information on what topics the teacher needs to discuss further in class. It is necessary for teachers to read the journals so the students know that the teachers are holding them accountable for content.

Teach Backs

In teach backs, students use the knowledge and skills they have learned to help other students learn the same thing. Teach backs reinforce what students have learned and facilitate peer interaction and support. Figure 4 can be used for assessment of a teach back. After teachers give initial performance feedback to the class, such as, "Everyone, don't forget to keep kicking when you take a breath," students may think they are kicking and ignore the reminder. If individual students are teaching other students, students are learning in several ways. The student doing the teaching is reviewing what he or she already knows. The student being taught is gaining additional information. Students can tell their partners, "I didn't see you kick," which allows those swimming to apply that information directly to their performances.

When assessing the student who is teaching, teachers should consider the following questions:

- Is the correct information being provided?
- Does the teaching student answer questions?

Teach Back Assessment

Name of Student _____   Teach Back Topic _____

Place a check in the "Yes" column to indicate appropriate teaching. Write comments in the "Needs Improvement" column to identify weaknesses that need attention.

	Yes	Needs Improvement
Knowledge/Performance		
Terminology was used correctly.		
Concepts were accurate.		
Skills were demonstrated accurately.		
Concepts were correctly linked to skills.		
Application of knowledge/skills was correct.		
Safety		
Teach back was conducted safely.		
Participants followed pool rules.		
Teaching student included safety warnings.		
Total Score _____		

Scoring—Give the student one point for each check in the "Yes" column. The better the technique is, the higher the score will be. Items marked for improvement should receive special attention during subsequent teach backs.

(Steffen & Grosse, 2003, p.21)

Figure 4. Teach Back Assessment

- Is the demonstration being performed correctly?
- Does the teaching student give helpful learning hints?
- Is the student being taught engaged in the experience and improving his or her knowledge and/or skill?
- Are safety procedures being followed?
- Does the teaching student convey safety warnings (if appropriate)?

Teach backs can demonstrate cognitive understanding to lower-skilled students. In addition, teachers can assess how well students have learned a skill by watching a student teach that skill to others. Teach backs can also demonstrate student misunderstanding or misinformation. If multiple students make the same mistake, teachers should realize that they need to re-teach that skill. Examples of several appropriate teach backs include:

- Teaching pool rules to a new student and/or pool guests.
- Teaching a surface dive to students who have missed class.
- Helping students practice or learn a skill.
- Asking higher-skilled students to teach specific skills to lesser-experienced students. This is particularly effective in large classes of students with varied abilities.
- Reviewing specific units of instruction prior to final testing and/or exams. For example, a student could call out names of different strokes and check to see if the swimmer performed the correct stroke, which demonstrates knowledge of stroke names and general performance of the stroke.
- Assisting a student with a disability. Teach backs are used frequently to assist individuals who may need additional help in learning swimming skills.

PART 3

Implementation of Assessment

When To Assess

Generally, teachers use formative assessment before starting new activities and during instruction. Summative assessment is used following instruction and practice in order to evaluate students' progress toward goals. While formal assessment can be implemented at any time, there are points at which specific assessments are more meaningful.

- Before starting an instructional swim class.
- After concept lessons to determine whether students have internalized and can apply appropriate concepts.
- After safety lessons to document what the instructor taught and to determine how well students learned the concepts.
- During skill progression classes.
- At the end of an instructional swim course or unit.

Before starting an instructional swim class, it is important for teachers to determine students' existing skill and knowledge levels. Student skill levels can range from nonswimmers to advanced swimmers. Without some precourse assessment, instructors may find it difficult to determine an appropriate and safe starting point for instruction.

If instructors use precourse assessments to determine students' deep-water competency, that assessment will help teachers decide whether to start the class in deep or shallow water.

In order to help students set swimming goals, teachers can combine precourse assessments with skill checklists. By comparing students' current abilities with the skills and knowledge covered in class, students are able to set their own goals and monitor their progress not only on a class-by-class basis, but also throughout the entire course. This assessment combination and goal-setting plan helps students develop skills and relate their abilities to a broader spectrum of swim skills. This practice will also allow students to continue learning swim skills after the completion of the swimming unit.

After concept lessons, teachers may want to assess how well students have assimilated the knowledge and concepts. This is especially crucial when basic swimming concepts (i.e., buoyancy, center of buoyancy, water resistance), safety information, and warnings are covered.

After safety lessons, to minimize liability issues—specifically a teacher's failure to warn students of danger—swimming teachers must document their dissemination of safety information to all students. Teachers also need to assess how well students understand that safety information. Written tests can assess students' comprehension of issues such as safety rules, appropriate behavior in an aquatic setting, and general class procedures. For example, swimming with closed eyes is a safety hazard. Students need to understand the danger and the potential consequences (e.g., head trauma from swimming into a wall or spinal injury from colliding with another swimmer) of swimming with their eyes closed.

During skill-progression classes, it is important to assess students' skills and their abilities to perform those skills. Skill development in swimming, as in all physical activities, is progressive. For example, swimmers' mastery of shallow-water skills are usually developed before deep–water skills. Swimmers develop breathing skills before they develop endurance; therefore, they are able to swim short distances before they can swim long distances.

When instructors combine skill checklists with skill/application assessments and goal-setting plans, they get an accurate picture of student achievement. These integrated assessments provide information on what a student can do in isolation (e.g., perform a surface dive) and when a sequence of skills is needed (e.g., swim to a specific point, perform a surface dive, pick up an object from the bottom of the pool, surface with the object, and carry the object to the side of the pool). If the sequence is the goal, teachers will need to be certain that students can master the individual skills (formative), as well as have the ability to perform the entire sequence (summative).

Assessment during skill progressions also brings to light the skills that need to be reviewed and further practiced. Scenarios, placed intermittently throughout the course, help to monitor students' abilities to make decisions and apply their knowledge. Learning a skill is not enough; students must also develop a decision-making process to decide when to use the acquired skill in order for mastery of that skill to be most valuable.

At the end of an instructional swim course or unit, teachers should assess students' exit knowledge, skills, and capabilities. Documenting achievement through skill checklists, combined skill tests/applications, written tests, scenarios, journals, and teach backs can help teachers build their students' self-esteem. These assessments can motivate students to continue participating in swimming and minimize the chance that students will overestimate their abilities, which could put them in potentially dangerous situations.

Assessment Options for Individuals with Disabilities

Many students with mild and/or moderate disabilities taking swim courses can participate in the same assessments as their class peers, and it is important they do so. If an Individualized Education Program (IEP) is in place, selection of activities should be appropriate to the goals documented in the IEP. Where this is the case, assessment takes on the added function of determining progress toward IEP goals. Because progress of special population students may be slower than that of peers their same age, it may be necessary to break skills down into smaller components.

In Appendix F are the Progression Chart for Students with Severe Disabilities and the Halliwick Method Skill Progression Chart. Both contain more detailed breakdowns of entry-level swim-skill progressions. These checklists are also useful for students who are unprepared for standard instructional swim progressions.

Teachers may want to use the Progression Chart for Students with Severe Disabilities and the Halliwick Method Skill Progression Chart in Appendix F to get more-detailed breakdowns of entry-level swim-skill progressions. The Progression Chart for Students with Severe Disabilities is based on standard learn-to-swim program skills, but with task progressions in smaller increments. The Halliwick Method Skill Progression Chart contains skills in the order they are used in the Halliwick method (an instructional program specifically designed for teaching swimming to individuals with

disabilities). Teachers can use either checklist, both of which allow for varying levels of independence. When students complete skills on these lists, they will have sufficient swimming skills to use the same skill checklists as their nondisabled peers.

Teachers may want to use other accommodations in order to assess swimmers with disabilities. Instructors may:

- Allow oral, rather than written, responses on written tests.
- Read written directions, scenarios, and tests.
- Provide tests or scenarios on videotape, audiotape, or computer, rather than in print.
- Ask the student to teach back to the teacher.
- Provide demonstrations or pictures, as well as verbal directions, during skill assessments.
- Provide additional verbal prompts during combined skill tests/applications.
- Assess skills at a time when the pool is less crowded or noisy. This reduces impeding wave action of the water and minimizes auditory and visual distractions.
- Allow additional time to complete assessment tasks.

Implementation Problems

Noise levels, venue suitability for written work, and wide variation in student abilities can all complicate assessment. Instructors must consider all of these challenges before they administer assessments.

High noise levels, which include participant noise and background noise from gutters and vents, inhibit hearing. In addition, when swimmers get water in their ears, they have more trouble hearing. In order to make sure students are able to hear the teacher's feedback, teachers may want to:

- Be sure that both the student and teacher are out of the water and standing a couple feet away from the side of the pool. Of course, during these moments, a lifeguard would be watching the other swimmers in the water.
- Provide additional written notes to students, following a verbal discussion.
- Have a follow-up conversation with a specific student or students after class.
- Assess students in pairs. One student can be swimming, while the second student is standing on the deck with the teacher. The teacher can provide verbal information to the second student, who relays it to the swimmer once the

teacher has moved on. After this procedure, the paired students can continue using teach backs for error correction.

Written assessments may be difficult in swim class. For written assessments, teachers may want to:

- Use poolside bleachers as desks. Students can sit backwards on the bleacher bench and use the higher bleacher above them as a writing surface.

- Ask students to complete their written assessments at the beginning of class. Students can enter the pool area, perform the assessment, turn in papers or take papers to their locker, and then shower and continue the lesson in the water.

- Use kickboards as writing surfaces. This is an alternative to bleachers, that is particularly useful if students must sit on a wet deck, without a place to write.

- Distribute or collect papers before students take showers prior to entering the pool. If students are writing in class, teachers may want to keep a box of pencils or pens near the poolside. When students enter the locker rooms to shower, teachers can collect their papers. For after-class paper distribution, teachers can meet students after they have dressed at a pre-arranged hallway location.

- Schedule a session in a traditional classroom periodically. By moving the entire group to an area conducive to reading, writing, and viewing videos, teachers are able to include a greater variety of assessments, answer questions, teach concepts, and reinforce safety.

- Have a variety of assessments ready to use during times when it is not possible to use the pool because of technical problems or short-ened class periods.

- Give assessments as homework. While some assessments, such as written tests that assess pool rules and class procedures, are best given in class. Other assessments, such as scenarios and journals, can be assigned as homework.

Assessing Multi-Ability Classes

Physical education swim classes are not always made up of students with similar abilities, which can complicate assessment. Instructors can individualize assessments by considering students' existing skills and their progress toward predeter-

mined goals. When teachers assess students in multi-ability classes, it helps to:

- Have a certified lifeguard on duty at all times, as recommended by the Aquatic Council of the American Association for Active Lifestyles and Fitness (1994) and the American Red Cross (2003, 2004a, 2004b, & 2004c). This provides continuous surveillance of the students.

- Have students within the same ability groups practice or engage in teach backs while the teacher assesses other ability groups.

- Ask higher–skilled students who are comfortable in deep water to help assess students learning in shallow water.

Conclusion

When teaching swimming, outcomes are to foster students' skill development and increase their swim knowledge. Ideally, students will learn to be safe in, on, and around water throughout their entire lives. Assessment should reveal the extent to which students have accomplished their goals and what work is still needed. Assessment should help teachers determine:

- What skills students can perform efficiently.

- How much students know about applying their acquired skills to accomplish specific tasks and maintain personal safety.

- Whether students have developed sound decision-making processes in an aquatic environment.

- Whether students' behaviors make participating in swimming a pleasurable, lifelong, health-enhancing activity.

Instructors need to use a variety of tools to assess student learning throughout an instructional swim unit or course. Students must be involved in the assessment process in order to clarify the links between personal abilities and decision-making in all areas of aquatic participation. Students who develop swimming skills build a foundation for lifelong aquatic participation. Instructors who creatively and accurately assess swimming skills have the potential to enrich students' entire learning process.

Appendix A. Aquatic Precourse Assessment Survey

The purpose of this questionnaire is to determine what you think your aquatic experience and abilities are as of now. Having this information will assist you in setting your goals and planning appropriate class activities for the coming course.

Each statement below describes swim abilities. Read all the statements and place a check next to the statement that best describes your present abilities.

_____ I can't swim at all.

_____ I can swim a little, as long as I stay where I can stand up.

_____ I can swim a little in deep water, as long as I can swim on my stomach.

_____ I can swim a little in deep water, on my back as well as my stomach.

_____ I am a strong, confident deep-water swimmer.

Which swim strokes do you know? Place a check next to each stroke you know and can swim at least 25 yards (one length of the pool).

____ front crawl	____ back crawl	____ sidestroke
____ breaststroke	____ butterfly	____ elementary backstroke

Can you pass a deep-water swim test without stopping, standing, or grabbing the side of the pool (i.e., jump into deep water, swim on your stomach 25 yards, reverse, swim 25 yards on your back to return to start)?

____ yes   ____ no

Read the Aquatic Skills Progression Chart (Appendix C). It lists all of the activities we may be doing in this course. Each column represents a different group of skills. Red skills progress to Orange, Orange to Yellow, Yellow to Green, and Green to Blue. If you can do all of the skills for a certain level, you would be on the next skill level to the right. Which skill group best represents the swim level you are currently on?

_____

_____

Which level do you think you should start on for this course? If you are confident of your skills, you may want to start with a level that has mostly new skills. If you feel you need more practice or review, you may want to select a level of skills you know, but on which you would like additional work.

_____

_____

Do you have any medical condition that might affect your participation in this course?

_____

_____

Is there anything else you would like me to know about you in order to help you succeed in this course?

_____

_____

Appendix B. Form Assessment Chart

Use this chart to document assessment of swim strokes. It can be utilized in several ways. To provide positive feedback, place a check next to aspects of a stroke a student performs appropriately. To indicate errors, circle specific items that need improvement.

Stroke	Arms	Legs	Coordination	Breathing

Front Crawl
Pass _____
	Alternate
	Over-water recovery
	High elbow
	Forward reach entry
	Over-water recovery
	"S" pull
		Alternating kick
		Full leg use
		Relaxed knees and
		  ankles
		No splash
			Continual kick	Rhythmic
				One breath every
				  one to two strokes
				Head turns to side
				Make bubbles when
				  face is in water

Back Crawl Pass _____	Alternate Thumb leads recovery Straight-arm recovery 11 and 1 entry Question mark pull	Alternating kick Full leg use Relaxed knees and ankles No splash	Continual kick	Natural

Elementary Backstroke
Pass _____
	Hands to armpits
	No higher than
	  shoulders to start pull
	Complete pull to side
		Heels outside knees
		Knees remain
		  underwater
		Power on snap
			Arms and legs
			  simultaneous
			Glide
				Natural

Breaststroke
Pass _____
	Hour-glass pull
	  Recover to chin
	Full extension in glide
		Heels outside knees
		No splash
		Power on snap
			Legs bend as arms
			  start recovery
			Streamlined glide,
			  face in
				One breath on every
				  pull
				Bubble on glide

Sidestroke
Pass _____
	Full, opposite
	  extension in glide
	Bottom arm pulls
	  parallel to top of
	  water
	Top arm stays close
	  to body
		Knees together
		  on bend
		Extension on "splits"
		Power on snap
			Arms and legs
			  simultaneous
			Streamlined glide,
			  ear resting on
			  bottom arm
				Natural

Butterfly Pass _____	Simultaneous Keyhole pull Over-water recovery High elbows	Legs together Hip "pop" Full leg/hip action	Kick at start and end of each pull	One breath at completion of every other pull or one breath every two strokes (swimmer's choice)

Appendix C. Aquatic Skills Progression Charts and Checklists

Aquatic Skills Progression Chart

	Red	Orange	Yellow
1*	Enter pool	Front kick 15 yards	Front crawl arms with rhythmic breathing (standing
2	Assume safe position	Back kick 15 yards	Front crawl with rhythmic breathing 15 yards
3	Maintain safe position	Front crawl arms standing	Back crawl arms standing
4	Wash face	Front crawl arms standing	Back crawl arms and kick 15 yards
5	Hold breath	Rhythmic breathing at the side of the pool	Elementary backstroke kick 15 yards
6	Submerge face	Combined stroke on front 15 yards	Elementary backstroke arms 15 yards
7	Submerge body	Finning	Deep-water bobs (10 repetitions)
8	Blow bubbles	Combined stroke on back 15 yards	Jump into deep water and swim 10 yards on front
9	Open eyes underwater	Lateral roll (front to back)	Jump into deep water, swim 10 yards yards on front, reverse (vertical rotation) and kick on back to return to start
10	Hold breath/submerge three seconds	Lateral roll (back to front)	Underwater swim 10 yards in three feet of water
11	Retrieve object in three feet of water	Vertical rotation (front float to back float)	Retrieve object in five feet of water
12	Supported front float	Vertical rotation (back float to front float)	Capsize small craft while wearing a PFD.
13	Supported front flutter kick	Jump into waist-deep water	Capsize craft while wearing a PFD and assume a safe resting position
14	Bobs with bubbles (10 repetitions) at side	Unsupported bobs with bubbles (10 repetitions)	Paddle capsized craft to safety
15	Front float and recovery	Feet-first surface dive	Perform primary survey and adult rescue breathing
16	Back float and recovery	Assist unbalanced swimmer to stand	Release of cramp
17	Back flutter kick	Reaching assists using arm, leg, towel, pole/object	Demonstrate U-turn change of direction
18	Use of PFD	Deep-water orientation	Throwing equipment rescue
19	Pool safety rules		
20	Exit pool over the side of the pool		

*Note: Numbers do not indicate order of difficulty. They are merely place holders to assist in using this form.

Green	Blue	White
Breaststroke kick supported	Scissor kick supported	Dolphin kick supported
Breaststroke arms standing	Sidestroke arms standing	Butterfly arms standing
Breaststroke combined arms and legs 15 yards	Sidestroke combined arms and legs 15 yards	Butterfly arms and breathing 15 yards
Breaststroke arms and breathing standing	Breaststroke 25 yards	Butterfly 15 yards
Breaststroke 15 yards.	Front crawl 50 yards	Front crawl 100 yards
Front crawl with rhythmic breathing 25 yards	Back crawl 50 yards	Back crawl 100 yards
Back crawl 25 yards	Long shallow dive	Breaststroke 100 yards
Kneeling dive	Feet-first surface dive to a depth of seven feet and swim underwater for 10 yards	Sidestroke 100 yards
Standing dive	Tuck surface dive and underwater swim 10 yards	10 minute swim using four different strokes
Standing dive and swim 25 yards stroke of choice	Survival float one minute	Flip turns back and front
Jump or dive, swim 10 yards, lateral roll to opposite body surface, and swim additional 10 yards	Jump into deep water and swim 25 yards wearing long pants, long-sleeved shirt, and light tennis shoes	Clearing mask and snorkel
Tread water 30 seconds	Disrobe in shallow water	Pike surface dive
Stride jump	Jump into deep water, swim for three minutes, and disrobe in deep water	Retrieve object from nine feet of water
HELP huddle positions	Disrobe, tread, and inflate clothing and use for flotation	Retrieve a 10-lb. brick from nine feet of water
Tuck surface dive	Five-minute continuous swim, choice of stroke	Tread water, no hands for five minutes
Adult CPR	Five-minute swim using front crawl, sidestroke, or breaststroke	Diving board safety
Closed turns for change of direction	Child and Infant CPR	Jump from diving board
Sculling (in place, feet first, head first)	Overhead, feet first sculling	Standing dive from board
Ice safety and rescue	Spinal injury safety and rescue	

Safety/Self Rescue Skills Progression Chart

	Personal Safety	Self Rescue	Rescue of Others
1	Safe participation guidelines	Face in float and recovery	Assist swimmer to stand
2	Maintain safe position in water	Float on back for three minutes	Arm assist from dick
3	Sunburn precautions	Release of cramp	Arm/leg assist from side of pool in water
4	Cold-weather precautions	Survival float for three minutes	Towel assist from deck
5	Environmental precautions (weather, marine life, currents, rip tides)	Roll from stomach to back while swimming	Pole assist from deck
6	Alcohol/drug use	Disrobing	Throwing rescue
7	Medical contraindications	Using clothes for flotation	Wading rescue
8	Buddy systems	Small craft capsize, rest, and self rescue	Emergency response
9	Personal limitations	Ice rescue	Cardiopulmonary resuscitation
10	Use of PFD	Tread water for two minutes	Ice rescue
11	Role of lifeguards	Tread water for two minutes without arm use	Call 911

Master Skills Checklist

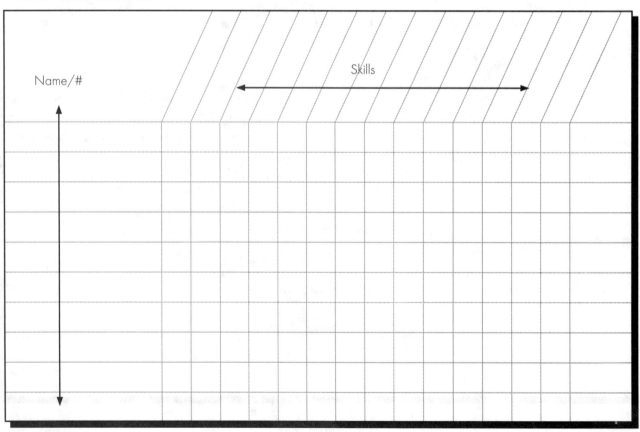

Appendix D. Combined Skill Tests/Applications

Assessing skill combinations and applications is important at all levels of aquatic learning. The following list of samples begins with very easy combinations/applications and progresses to more complex examples. Students can also design their own combinations in order to demonstrate competencies they wish to substantiate.

- In chest-deep water of uniform depth, walk 20 steps forward, turn around, and run back to the starting point.

- In chest-deep water of uniform depth, walk forward 10 yards, alternating four steps with two complete submersions with bubbles. Walk backward to return to start.

- In chest-deep water of uniform depth, walk forward six steps, push off into a front glide with kick. When a breath is needed roll onto back and rest and breathe. Stand and walk to return to start.

- Swim on stomach a distance of at least 10 yards. Start with face in water and either take breaths as needed or use rhythmic breathing. Reverse direction without standing and swim on back to return to start.

- Jump into shallow water, level off, and swim 10 yards. Roll to back and continue to swim an additional 10 yards.

- Swim in a circle a distance of 20 yards, reverse and swim the circle in the opposite direction an additional 20 yards.

- In chest-deep water of uniform depth, submerge feet first until at the bottom. Roll forward and stretch to a position with stomach on the bottom of the pool. Swim three body lengths on the bottom. Surface and continue to swim another five yards.

- Jump into deep water, surface, and tread one minute, then swim (any stroke) a distance of 10 yards.

- Dive into at least nine feet of water, take three strokes underwater, surface, and swim 20 yards.

- Swim 20 yards, get out onto the deck, and use an extension rescue device to assist a tired swimmer.

- Jump into deep water, surface, and swim 20 yards on stomach. Reverse without touching bottom and swim on back to return to start.

- Swim 20 yards on stomach. Reverse and swim 10 yards on back. Release cramp in foot. Swim any stroke to return to start.

Appendix E. Written Tests

Written Test to Document Safety and Pool Rules Knowledge

Note: Answers are provided in parentheses.

Section 1—*Fill in the blank.* For each statement below, complete the statement by adding the word or words that best completes the statement.

1. Before entering the pool area, it will help keep the pool cleaner if I (SHOWER).
2. Before I can swim in deep water I must (PASS A SWIM TEST).
3. When entering shallow water I should enter (FEET FIRST) or (AT THE LADDER).
4. The minimum safe depth for diving head first into the pool is (9 FEET).
5. If I dive into shallow water I could (DIE) or (BECOME PARALYZED) or (BE SERIOUSLY HURT).
6. Any day I cannot participate in swim class I must (BRING A WRITTEN EXCUSE).
7. On swimming days I must have what supplies? (SWIM SUIT, CAP, TOWEL).
8. A whistle means (STOP, LOOK, AND LISTEN IMMEDIATELY).
9. If I miss a class, either because I am absent or because I am excused I (HAVE TO MAKE UP CLASS DURING OPEN SWIM).
10. When moving around on deck I should (WALK) at all times.

Section 2— *True or False.* For each statement below, decide if the information is true or false. Circle the correct letter. If the information is false, correct the statement on the line below.

11. T F It is all right to dive into shallow water providing you come up quickly. (IT IS NEVER ALL RIGHT TO DIVE INTO SHALLOW WATER.)

12. T F I can go into deep water as long as I hang onto the side. (I MUST PASS A SWIM TEST TO GO INTO DEEP WATER.)

13. T F If I dive into shallow water I won't be seriously hurt. (I COULD INJURE MYSELF OR EVEN DIE.)

14. T F Even if I took a bath the day before, I should shower before entering the pool. _____

15. T F If I cannot participate, I still must put on my suit and watch. _____

16. T F If I cannot participate, I will not have to make up the work if I have a good excuse. (ALL MISSED PARTICIPATION MUST BE MADE UP.)

17. T F A whistle means I have 5 more minutes to swim. (A WHISTLE MEANS STOP, LOOK, AND LISTEN IMMEDIATELY.)

18. T F It is ok to grab onto someone else if I really need to or want to talk to them. (I MUST KEEP MY HANDS TO MYSELF AT ALL TIMES.)

19. T F I cannot bring any food or drink into the pool area. _____

20. T F During a fire drill we have to exit the building just like everyone else. _____

_____

Section 3—*Essay.* Describe your current swim level. Where in the pool are you allowed to swim? What knowledge and abilities do you have? What do you want to learn in this class? (ANSWER SHOULD BE APPROPRIATE FOR INDIVIDUAL STUDENT BASED ON PRECOURSE ASSESSMENT.)

Written Test to Document Knowledge of Swim Strokes

Note: Answers are provided in parentheses.

Section 1—*Fill in the blank.* For each statement below, complete the statement by adding the word or words that best completes the statement.

1. The stroke in which you take a breath by turning your head to the side is the (FRONT CRAWL).
2. The stroke in which your arms pull first, and then you kick and glide is the (BREASTSTROKE).
3. The skill used to get to the bottom of the pool is the (SURFACE DIVE).
4. The best stroke for resting while you swim is the (ELEMENTARY BACKSTROKE).
5. The stroke with a Dolphin kick is the (BUTTERFLY).
6. The stroke usually used for swimming under water is the (BREASTSTROKE).
7. The fastest racing stroke is the (FRONT CRAWL).
8. The only racing stroke on the back is the (BACK CRAWL).
9. The stroke with a scissors kick is the (SIDESTROKE).

Section 2—Following are specific swim strokes. Under each stroke, write the name of that stroke.

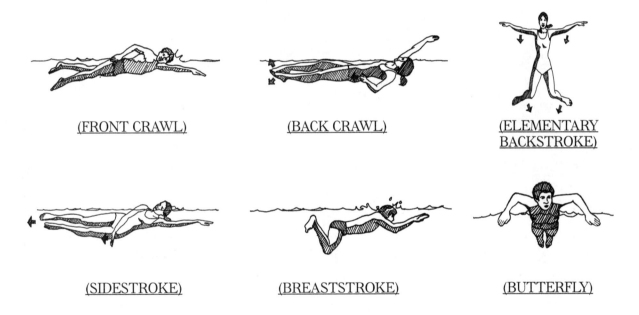

(FRONT CRAWL) (BACK CRAWL) (ELEMENTARY BACKSTROKE)

(SIDESTROKE) (BREASTSTROKE) (BUTTERFLY)

Section 3—List five (5) hints you would give to someone to keep them from getting tired while swimming.

APPROPRIATE ANSWERS:
1. Use rhythmic breathing.
2. Swim at an even pace and do not rush.
3. Change strokes periodically.
4. Use a resting stroke.
5. Be sure to glide, if the stroke you are swimming has a glide.

Appendix F. Progress Chart for Students with Severe Disabilities and the Halliwick-Method Skill Progression Chart

Progression Chart for Students with Severe Disabilities (Grosse & Sparrow, 1990)

	Water Orientation Assisted	Water Orientation Unassisted	Pre-Beginner
1	Enter pool	Enter pool	Water adjustment
2	Assume safe position	Assume safe position	Breath holding
3	Maintain safe position	Maintain safe position	10 bobs with bubbles
4	Wash face	Wash face	Prone float and recovery
5	Breath holding	Breath holding	Prone glide
6	Blowing bubbles on water	Blowing bubbles on water	Back glide and recovery
7	Face in water	Face in water	Prone glide with propulsion
8	Blow bubbles with face in water	Blow bubbles with face in water	Back glide with propulsion
9	Bobs	Bobs	Beginner stroke or crawl for four body lengths
10	Open eyes in water	Open eyes in water	Combined stroke on back for four body lengths
11	Assisted prone float and recovery	Unassisted prone float and assisted recovery	Leveling off and swimming
12	Back float and recovery assist	Unassisted back float and assisted recovery	Jump or fall into shallow water
13	Leg action with support	Leg action with support	Changing position (vertical)
14	Arm action with support	Arm action with support	Turning over (horizontal)
15	Leg action and bubbles	Leg action and bubbles	Release of cramp
16	Arm action and bubbles	Arm action and bubbles	Nonswimmer assist
17	Safety skills	Safety skills	Reaching and extension rescues
18			Use of a PFD
19			Artificial respiration
20			Safety skills

Halliwick Method Skill Progression Chart (Grosse, 2001)

Category	Performance Level*		
Skill	Assisted & Cued	Cued	Independent
Water Entry			
Seated position on side			
Fall forward into water			
Assume safe position			
Maintain safe position			
Assume position at side			
Maintain position at side			
Maintain side position for one minute			
Enter from wheelchair**			
Locomotion			
Walk forward			
Kangaroo jump forward			
Bicycle forward			
Run forward			
Walk backward			
Walk sideward			
Breathing			
Hold breath, face out			
Blow out, face out			
Hold breath, face in			
Blow out on water			
Blow out, face in			
Blow bubbles for 10 seconds			
Blow bubbles for 20 seconds**			
Lateral Roll			
Supine float			
Head turn 90 degrees to the right			
Head turn 90 degrees to the left			
Head turn right and return			
Head turn left and return			
Return to supine after tip right			
Return to supine after tip left			
Right roll and return			
Left roll and return			
Full roll to right**			
Full roll to left**			

* Assisted and cued means needing physical assistance and verbal cue.
 Cued means needing verbal cue only.
 Independent means no physical assistance or verbal cue needed.
** Advanced activity

| Category | Performance Level* | | |
Skill	Assisted & Cued	Cued	Independent
Vertical Roll			
Head tilt backward			
Head tilt forward			
Head tilt to supine float			
Head tilt forward to bubble			
Head tile backward to fwd			
Head tilt to prone float			
Head lift from prone float			
Vertical to prone float			
Prone float to vertical			
Vertical to supine float			
Supine float to vertical			
Supine to prone**			
Prone to supine**			
Submersion			
Make bubbles 10 seconds			
Prone dunk in four inches of water and recovery			
Prone dunk in one foot of water and recovery			
Prone dunk in two feet of water and recovery**			
Short toss and recovery**			
Fall in from deck and recovery**			
Group Activities			
Snake			
Circle holding arms			
Lateral rolls around circle**			
Object passing in supine			
Object passing in vertical			
Turbulence			
Supine float			
Supine float with slight turbulence			
Supine float with waves**			
Swim Progression			
Prone mobility**			
Supine mobility**			
Water Exit			
Push up on side			
Prone position over side of the pool			
Roll on deck sit**			

*   Assisted and cued means needing physical assistance and verbal cue.
    Cued means needing verbal cue only.
    Independent means no physical assistance or verbal cue needed.
** Advanced activity

REFERENCES

American Association for Active Lifestyles and Fitness. (1994). *Safety in high school physical education aquatic programs* [Position paper]. Reston, VA: Author.

American Red Cross. (2003). *Lifeguard training.* St. Louis. Staywell.

American Red Cross. (2004a). *Guide for training American Red Cross water safety instructors.* Washington, DC: Author.

American Red Cross. (2004b). *Swimming & water safety.* St. Louis: Staywell.

American Red Cross. (2004c). *Water safety instructor's manual.* St. Louis: Staywell.

Bayless, M. A., & Adams, S. H. (1985). A liability checklist. *Journal of Physical Education, Recreation & Dance, 56*(2), 49.

Colvin, C. M.(1992). *Swimming into the 21st century.* Champaign, IL: Human Kinetics.

Grosse, S. (2001). *The Halliwick method: Water freedom for individuals with disabilities.* Milwaukee: Aquatic Consulting & Education Resource Services.

Grosse, S., & Sparrow, C. (1990). New course certifications provide opportunity in adapted aquatics. *National Aquatic Journal, 6*(2), 7-9.

McEvoy, J. E. (1993). *Swim your way to fitness.* Mechanicsburg, PA: Stackpole.

Meeks, C. (1990). The legal duties of a coach. *Indiana AHPERD Journal, 19*(2), 39-42.

National Association for Sport and Physical Education. (1995). *Moving into the future: National standards for physical education: A guide to content and assessment.* Reston, VA: Author.

National Association for Sport and Physical Education. (2004). *Moving into the future: National standards for physical education* (2nd ed.). Reston, VA: Author.

Steffen, J., & Grosse, S. J.(2003). *Assessment in outdoor adventure physical education.* Reston, VA: National Association for Sport and Physical Education.

Thomas, D. G. (1989) *Teaching swimming: Steps to success.* Champaign, IL: Human Kinetics.

Wiggins, G., & McTighe, J. (1998). *Understanding by design.* Alexandria, VA: Association for Supervision and Curriculum Development.

YMCA of the USA. (1999). *Youth and adult aquatics program manual.* Champaign, IL: Human Kinetics.

Published by the National Association for Sport and Physical Education for quality physical education programs:

Moving into the Future: National Standards for Physical Education, 2nd edition (2004), Stock No. 304-10275

Physical Educators' Guide to Successful Grant Writing (2005), Stock No. 304-10291

Ask-PE: Physical Education Concepts Test CD-ROM (2004), Stock No. 304-10271P & 304-10271M

Concepts and Principles of Physical Education: What Every Student Needs to Know (2003), Stock No. 304-10261

Beyond Activities: Elementary Volume (2003), Stock No. 304-10265

Beyond Activities: Secondary Volume (2003), Stock No. 304-10268

National Physical Education Standards in Action (2003), Stock No. 304-10267

On Your Mark... Get Set... Go!: A Guide for Beginning Physical Education Teachers (2004), Stock No. 304-10264

Physical Activity for Children: A Statement of Guidelines (2004), Stock No. 304-10276

National Standards for Beginning Physical Education Teachers (2003), Stock No. 304-10273

Active Start: A Statement of Physical Activity Guidelines for Children Birth to Five Years (2002), Stock No. 304-10254

Appropriate Practice Documents

Appropriate Practice in Movement Programs for Young Children (2000), Stock No. 304-10232

Appropriate Practices for Elementary School Physical Education (2000), Stock No. 304-10230

Appropriate Practices for Middle School Physical Education (2001), Stock No. 304-10248

Appropriate Practices for High School Physical Education (2004), Stock No. 304-10272

Opportunity to Learn Documents

Opportunity to Learn Standards for Elementary Physical Education (2000), Stock No. 304-10242

Opportunity to Learn Standards for Middle School Physical Education (2004), Stock No. 304-10290

Opportunity to Learn Standards for High School Physical Education (2004), Stock No. 304-10289

Assessment Series

Assessment of Swimming in Physical Education (2005), Stock No. 304-10301

Assessing Dance in Elementary Physical Education (2005), Stock No. 304-10304

Assessing Concepts: Secondary Biomechanics (2004), Stock No. 304-10220

Assessment in Outdoor Adventure Physical Education (2003), Stock No. 304-10218

Assessing Student Outcomes in Sport Education (2003), Stock No. 304-10219

Video Tools for Teaching Motor Skill Assessment (2002), Stock No. 304-10217

Assessing Heart Rate in Physical Education (2002), Stock No. 304-10214

Authentic Assessment of Physical Activity for High School Students (2002), Stock No. 304-10216

Portfolio Assessment for K-12 Physical Education (2000), Stock No. 304-10213

Elementary Heart Health: Lessons and Assessment (2001), Stock No. 304-10215

Standards-Based Assessment of Student Learning: A Comprehensive Approach (1999), Stock No. 304-10206

Assessment in Games Teaching (1999), Stock No. 304-10212

Assessing Motor Skills in Elementary Physical Education (1999), Stock No. 304-10207

Assessing and Improving Fitness in Elementary Physical Education (1999), Stock No. 304-10208

Creating Rubrics for Physical Education (1999), Stock No. 304-10209

Assessing Student Responsibility and Teamwork (1999), Stock No. 304-10210

Order online at www.naspeinfo.org or call 1-800-321-0789

Shipping and handling additional.

National Association for Sport and Physical Education, an association of the American Alliance for Health, Physical Education, Recreation, and Dance

1900 Association Drive, Reston, VA 20191, naspe@aahperd.org, 703-476-3410